day hikes

Acadia National Park

Help Us Keep This Guide Up to Date

Every effort has been made by the authors and editors to make this guide as accurate and useful as possible. However, many things can change after a guide is published—establishments close, phone numbers change, hiking trails are rerouted, facilities come under new management, etc.

We would love to hear from you concerning your experiences with this guide and how you feel it could be improved and kept up to date. While we may not be able to respond to all comments and suggestions, we'll take them to heart and we'll also make certain to share them with the authors. Please send your comments and suggestions to the following address:

The Globe Pequot Press

Reader Response/Editorial Department

P.O. Box 480

Guilford, CT 06437

Or you may e-mail us at:

editorial@GlobePequot.com

Thanks for your input, and happy travels!

Best Easy Day Hikes Series

best
easy
day hikes
Acadia National Park

Dolores Kong
Dan Ring

FALCONGUIDES ®

GUILFORD, CONNECTICUT
HELENA, MONTANA

AN IMPRINT OF THE GLOBE PEQUOT PRESS

FALCONGUIDES®

Cover photo: Jim Schwabel/Index Stock

Library of Congress Cataloging-in-Publication Data

Kong, Dolores.
  Best easy day hikes Acadia National Park / Dolores Kong, Dan Ring. — 1st ed.
    p. cm. — (Best easy day hikes series) (A Falcon guide)
    ISBN 978-1-56044-441-1
    1. Hiking—Maine—Acadia National Park—Guidebooks. 2. Trails—Maine—Acadia National Park—Guidebooks. 3. Acadia National Park (Me.)—Guidebooks. I. Ring, Dan (Daniel) II. Title. III. Series. IV. Series: A Falcon guide

GV199.42.M22 A323 2001
917.41'450444—dc21

                                                                    200123664

Printed in the United States of America
First Edition/Fifth Printing

Contents

Acknowledgments

For showing us a side of Acadia that most people don't see, and for being so generous with their time, we'd like to thank Jim Vekasi, Gary Stellpflug, Chris Barter, Wayne Barter, John Cousins, Deb Wade, David Kari, Kristen Britain, and the rest of the Acadia National Park staff; Margie Coffin, landscape architect for the National Park Service's Olmsted Center for Landscape Preservation; and Marla Major, associate conservation director for Friends of Acadia. We'd also like to thank Dianne Dumanoski and Carlo Obligato, Carol Stocker, and Robert Mussey, for sharing with us their love of nature and history.

Map Legend

Interstate Highway/Freeway	(15)	Ranger Station		♠
US Highway	(66)	Campground		△
State or Other Principal Road	(47) (190)	Picnic Area		⊼
Forest Road	416	Building		■
Interstate Highway	⟹	Peak		9,782 ft.
Paved Road	⟹	River/Creek		～
Gravel Road	⟹	Lake/Pond		⬭
Carriage Road	⟹	Breakwater		▬▬
Trailhead	◯	Ferry Line		-----
Parking Area	℗	Point of Interest		◙
Main Trail/Route	••-•~••	National Forest/Park Boundary		
Alternate/Secondary Trail/Route	---~/\---	Map Orientation		N ⬧
One Way Road	One Way →	Scale		0 0.5 1
City	Bar Harbor ◯			Miles

ix

Overview Map
Mount Desert Island East of Somes Sound

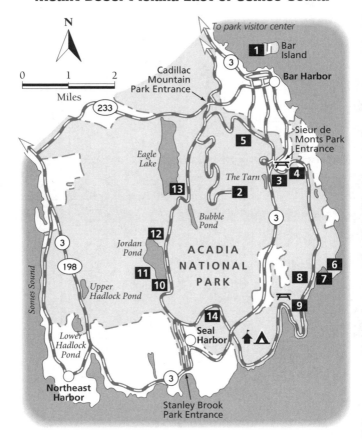

Overview Map
Mount Desert Island West of Somes Sound

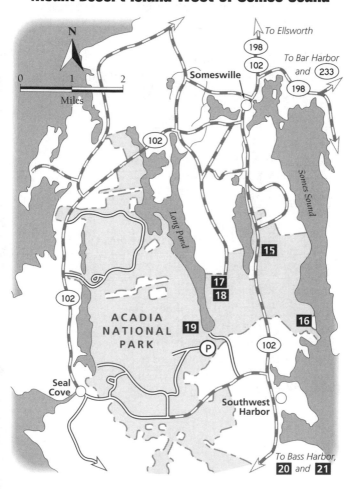

Ranking the Hikes

The following list ranks the hikes in this book from easiest to hardest.

Easiest
  1 Bar Island Trail
  2 Cadillac Summit Loop Trail
  5 Jesup Path (Great Meadow Loop)
  7 Ocean Path
10 Jordan Pond Nature Trail
20 Wonderland Trail
21 Ship Harbor Nature Trail
11 Jordan Pond Shore Trail
17 Beech Cliff Trail
13 Eagle Lake Trail
19 Great Pond Trail
  6 Sand Beach and Great Head Trail
  3 Beachcroft Trail
  4 Bear Brook Trail
  8 The Bowl Trail
  9 Gorham Mountain Trail
12 Bubble Rock Trail
14 Day Mountain Trail
16 Flying Mountain Trail
18 Beech Mountain Trail

Hardest 15 Acadia Mountain Trail

Introduction

In Maine's Acadia National Park, you can see images found nowhere else, such as the surf crashing on pink granite cliffs or the fog rolling in over Frenchman Bay. With 120 miles of hiking trails and 45 miles of carriage roads throughout its approximately 40,000 acres, Acadia provides a wealth of opportunity to experience the many aspects of nature.

This guide is for those with limited time to enjoy Acadia, or for those who want to sample only the easiest or most popular trails. *Best Easy Day Hikes Acadia National Park* was researched as part of our more comprehensive guide, *Hiking Acadia National Park*.

While *Hiking Acadia National Park* covers nearly all of the park's trails, including those in the harder-to-reach parts of the park like Schoodic Peninsula, this guide includes just the best easy hikes in the main part of Acadia, on Mount Desert Island. Also excluded from this guide are the strenuous cliff climbs that are included in *Hiking Acadia National Park*.

Many of the trails described here are very easy and suitable for families with young children, but some are moderately difficult hikes that are among the most popular in the area, bringing you to grand mountaintop vistas. The "Ranking the Hikes" section of this guide offers a listing of these hikes by level of difficulty.

Even before Acadia was established as the first national park in the eastern United States in 1916, people were attracted by what the area had to offer. Native Americans, European settlers, nineteenth-century artists such as Thomas Cole and Frederic Church, and famous families including the Rockefellers, the Vanderbilts, and the Carnegies, all came here, lured by the region's beauty, mystery, and natural resources.

In fact, the extensive trail system includes Native American paths, old roads, and trails built by local Village Improvement Associations near the turn of the twentieth century.

To preserve this history, Acadia National Park, the National Park Service's Olmsted Center for Landscape Preservation, and Friends of Acadia began a major planning project for management, maintenance, and reconstruction of the trails in 1999. The project, estimated to take at least 10 years to complete, is being funded by a $4 million commitment from the National Park Service, and millions more in private matching funds.

Acadia's trail system is nominated for the National Register of Historic Places, and funding for trail maintenance comes from a variety of sources, including millions of dollars from individual donors and visitor fees. In 1999, federal officials announced that Acadia would become the first national park with trails maintained by a private endowment, Acadia Trails Forever, with funds raised in partnership with Friends of Acadia.

The 45 miles of carriage roads in Acadia are equally historic, constructed by Mount Desert Island summer resident John D. Rockefeller Jr., beginning in 1911. While the carriage roads are suitable for easy hikes, they are also used by bicyclists and horseback riders, and are not described in this guide.

Aside from hiking some of the trails described here, visitors may also want to stop at the Abbe Museum, the Wild Gardens of Acadia, and the Nature Center, all located at the Sieur de Monts entrance to the park, on Maine 3 south of Bar Harbor.

The Abbe Museum, founded by Dr. Robert Abbe, a pioneer of the medical use of radium, celebrates and preserves the culture and heritage of Native Americans who lived here thousands of years before European settlers set eyes on the Maine coast. In addition to the seasonal museum at the Sieur de Monts Spring entrance, a year-round museum facility is expected to open in 2001 in downtown Bar Harbor.

The Wild Gardens of Acadia and the Nature Center introduce the visitor to some of the flora and fauna of Acadia.

The park entrance fee is $10 per vehicle for a seven-day pass. From late June to Labor Day, a free Island Explorer shuttle bus operates between points on Mount Desert Island and the park.

—*Dolores Kong and Dan Ring*

Zero Impact

Going into a wild area is like visiting a famous museum. You obviously do not want to leave your mark on an art treasure in the museum. If everybody going through the museum left one little mark, the art would be destroyed quickly—and of what value is a big building full of trashed art? The same goes for pristine wildlands. If we all left just one little mark on the landscape, the backcountry would soon be spoiled.

Waste

Pack out all garbage and trash. If you can carry items in when they are full, you can carry them out empty. After your hike, dispose of trash at trailhead receptacles, if available, or in waste containers at a campground, rest area, or other facility.

Human waste must be disposed of carefully or it becomes a health hazard. Use restroom facilities at trailheads or along the trail. If absolutely necessary, select a site at least 100 yards from streams, lakes, springs, and other water sources. Dig a small "cat-hole" about 6 inches into the organic layer of the soil. (Some people carry a small plastic trowel for this purpose.) When finished, refill the hole, and make the site look as natural as possible. Land managers now recommend that all toilet paper be carried out. Use double zipper bags with a small amount of baking soda to absorb odor.

Stay on the Trail

Do not cut switchbacks or take other short cuts. This practice erodes trails, increases the cost of trail maintenance, and requires you to expend more energy than if you stay on the trail. If travelling cross-country, stay on pine needles, rock, sand, or gravel as much as you can, and spread your group out to avoid creating a new trail. Never construct tree blazes, rock cairns, or any other type of trail marker. Select durable surfaces, like rocks, logs, or sandy areas, for resting spots.

Animals and Plants

Do not feed wild animals—people food is very bad for them, and animals that become used to handouts lose their fear of humans and become nuisances that may have to be killed.

Never pick flowers, or gather plants or insects. So many people visit these trails that the cumulative effect of individual impacts can be great.

Keep your impact to a minimum by taking only pictures and leaving only footprints. The wildlife and the people who will pass this way another day are thankful for your courtesy.

Three Falcon Zero-Impact Principles

- *Leave with everything you brought.*
- *Leave no sign of your visit.*
- *Leave the landscape as you found it.*

Play It Safe

Whether a trail is very near civilization or more remote, you should be prepared for any weather and trail conditions you may encounter. These tips will help you make your trip safe and enjoyable.

Important Contact Information

Information about the park may be obtained by contacting Acadia National Park, P.O. Box 177, Bar Harbor, ME 04609. The telephone number is (207) 288-3338, and the website is www.nps.gov/acad/.

The Hulls Cove Visitor Center is located on Maine 3, northwest of Bar Harbor. It is open from 8 a.m. to 4 p.m. daily from mid-April through June, and in October. It is open from 8 a.m. to 6 p.m. daily in July and August. The daily hours vary in September.

The Winter Visitor Center is at Acadia National Park headquarters on Maine 233, west of Bar Harbor. It is open from 8 a.m. to 4:30 p.m. daily from November through mid-April, and is closed Thanksgiving Day, December 24 and 25, and January 1.

For schedules, route maps, and other information about the free Island Explorer bus shuttle, contact www.exploreacadia.com.

Hikers also might find the detailed United States Geological Survey map of the park helpful. The Acadia National Park and Vicinity map is available at the park's visitor center.

Water

Hikers generally need 1 or more quarts per person on these day hikes, depending on the weather. Do not count on finding water on any hike. If you use natural water sources, remember that all water should be treated with a water purifier or iodine tablets before consumption. It is easier and safer to carry all the water you will need from home or another potable water source.

Sun

To protect yourself from the potentially harmful effects of over-exposure to the sun, wear protective clothing and especially a sun hat. Use a sunscreen lotion with a sun protection factor of at least 30 for maximum protection against sunburn and the aging effects of sunlight. A tan does not make you immune to sunburn!

Hike Plan

Always tell a reliable person your hiking plans, especially if you will be hiking in the more remote areas. Stick to your plan when you are on the hike, and be sure to check in upon your return.

Other Considerations

- Pack a first-aid kit on each excursion.
- Dress in layers so that you are prepared for changes in temperature.
- Do not leave valuables in your car.
- Do not hike alone—there is safety in numbers.

Gear Every Hiker Should Carry
- Water
- Food
- Sun hat
- Sunscreen
- Sunglasses
- Durable hiking shoes or boots
- Synthetic fleece jacket or pullover
- Rain gear
- Map
- Compass
- First-aid kit
- Signal mirror
- Toilet paper and zippered plastic bags

Mount Desert Island East of Somes Sound

Most of Acadia National Park's trails, the main Park Loop Road, and many of the best views are here on the eastern half of Mount Desert Island. Most of the "best easy" hikes are also located here.

The various hikes in this section are grouped into three geographic divisions: the Bar Harbor, Cadillac, and Champlain Mountains area; the Gorham Mountain area; and the Jordan Pond, Bubbles, and Eagle Lake area.

From trails in the Bar Harbor, Cadillac, and Champlain Mountains area, you can get some of Acadia's best-known views of Bar Harbor, Frenchman Bay, and the Porcupine Islands. The park's Sieur de Monts entrance is also in this area, allowing access to the Wild Gardens of Acadia, the Nature Center, and the Abbe Museum.

The Gorham Mountain area features such seashore hikes as Sand Beach and Great Head Trail, and the very easy Ocean Path, as well as such moderately difficult hikes as the Gorham Mountain Trail.

At the heart of the Jordan Pond, Bubbles, and Eagle Lake area is the Jordan Pond House, famous for its afternoon tea and popovers, and its view of the distinctive Bubbles. The Jordan Pond House serves as a jumping-off point for several easy trails. Other dominant features accessible by trails in this area include a precariously perched rock known as Bubble Rock, and Eagle Lake.

9

BAR HARBOR, CADILLAC, AND CHAMPLAIN MOUNTAINS AREA

1
BAR ISLAND TRAIL

Highlights: A low-tide walk leads to a rocky island off Bar Harbor.
Type of hike: Out-and-back.
Total distance: 1.4 miles.
Map: USGS Acadia National Park and Vicinity.
Parking and trailhead facilities: There is limited on-street parking on West Street. All facilities can be found in town.

Finding the trailhead: From Maine 3 at the park visitor center, head south for about 2.5 miles, toward downtown Bar Harbor. Turn left (east) onto West Street, which is at the first intersection after the College of the Atlantic. The trail, visible only at low tide, leaves from Bridge Street, the first left off West Street on the edge of downtown.

Bar Island Trail

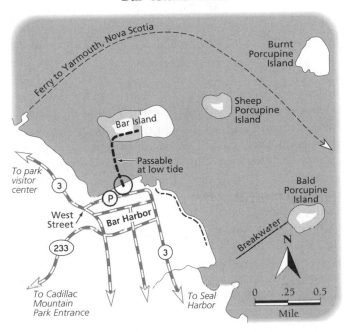

Key points:

0.0 Bar Island Trailhead.

0.3 Reach the shore of Bar Island; head northeast up the gravel road behind the gate.

0.5 At the junction, bear left (northeast) at the trail sign.

0.6 At the junction, bear right (southeast) up to the island's summit.

0.7 Reach the island's summit.

1.4 Return to the trailhead.

The hike: The Bar Island Trail is a short easy jaunt within shouting distance of Bar Harbor, but you feel transported to another world. That is the beauty of being on an island, even a small one so close to a busy summer resort town.

Easy enough for the least-seasoned hiker, the Bar Island Trail also provides a bit of risk to satisfy the thrill-seeking adventurer—it can only be traveled at low tide, when a gravel bar connecting Bar Harbor and the island is exposed. "Caution!" a sign warns hikers once they reach the island's rocky shores. "Safe crossing is 1.5 hours on either side of low tide. Check tide chart for daily tide time! Caution!" For your convenience, a tide chart is posted.

First described in 1867, the trail was reopened by the National Park Service in the 1990s. Parts of the island are still privately owned.

From the foot of Bridge Street in Bar Harbor, walk northwest across the gravel bar, reaching the island at about 0.3 mile. Some of the resort town's historic summer "cottages"—really mansions—are visible along Bar Harbor's shoreline to the left (southwest) as you cross the gravel bar.

Once you reach Bar Island, head northeast up the gravel road behind the gate. The trail soon levels off at a grassy field. At 0.5 mile, bear left (northeast) at a trail sign pointing into the woods toward Bar Island summit. At the fork at 0.6 mile, bear right (southeast) up a rocky knob.

At 0.7 mile, you reach the summit, with its old wooden flagpole and views toward Bar Harbor. From here, you can hear the town's church bells, see the fishing and recreational boats along the harbor, and take in the smells of the sea and the views of the mountains.

Return the way you came.

Option: Instead of taking the gravel road inland toward the summit, you can walk along the rocky shores on the western side of Bar Island, making it as long or as short a hike as you like.

Cadillac Summit Loop Trail

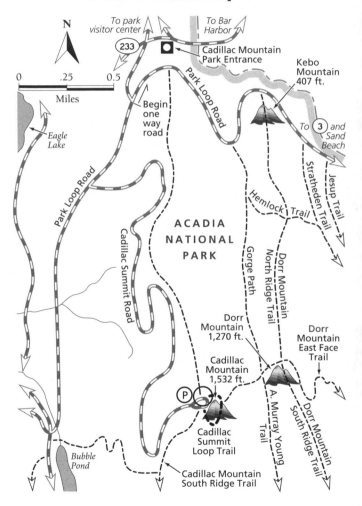

2
CADILLAC SUMMIT LOOP TRAIL

Highlights: This trail boasts spectacular views from Acadia's highest mountain and plaques with geological information.
Type of hike: Loop.
Total distance: 0.5 mile.
Map: USGS Acadia National Park and Vicinity.
Parking and trailhead facilities: Parking is available at the summit parking area. The gift shop and rest rooms are open in late spring to early summer. The walkway is partially wheelchair and baby-stroller accessible.

Finding the trailhead: From park visitor center, drive south on the Park Loop Road for about 3.5 miles and turn left (east) at the sign for Cadillac Mountain. Ascend the winding summit road to the top. The paved walkway leaves from behind the large pink granite boulder with the memorial plaque.

Key points:
0.0 Cadillac Summit Loop Trailhead.
0.5 Complete the loop at the trailhead.

The hike: You gain a new appreciation for Cadillac Mountain on this trail, with plaques describing the geology of

Mount Desert Island and the spectacular views from Acadia's highest summit, at 1,532 feet.

The loop trail leaves from the eastern edge of the parking area, behind a large pink granite boulder with a plaque in memory of Stephen Tyng Mather, who laid the foundation for the National Park Service.

The loop is best done in a clockwise direction, to follow the order of the descriptive plaques. The paved walkway, tinged to match the pink granite atop Cadillac Mountain, provides access to wheelchairs and baby strollers for about half of the loop. You are also free to stray off the walkway and on to the mountain's pink granite ledges, but it is best to stay on the path or solid rock to avoid trampling vegetation and causing soil erosion.

Because of its grand vistas of Frenchman Bay, the Porcupine Islands, and the other mountains of Acadia, as well as its easy accessibility, the loop trail can get very crowded in the summer. Early mornings and late afternoons are best, although the summit road is open one hour before sunrise for those wishing to catch the day's first rays, and does not close until midnight, for those wanting to see starlit skies and the lights of Bar Harbor.

Option: Ambitious hikers can descend steeply from the loop trail into the gorge east of Cadillac Mountain, and climb up lower Dorr Mountain, with its closer-up views of the ocean. The strenuous path connecting the two summits is 0.6 mile one-way. Return the same way.

3
BEACHCROFT TRAIL

Highlights: Intricately laid stone steps lead much of the way to open views along Huguenot Head and Champlain Mountain.

Type of hike: Out-and-back.

Total distance: 2.4 miles.

Map: USGS Acadia National Park and Vicinity.

Parking and trailhead facilities: Park at The Tarn parking lot on the right (west) side, of Maine 3. There are no facilities.

Finding the trailhead: From downtown Bar Harbor, head south on Maine 3 for about 2 miles to the park's Sieur de Monts entrance. Continue past the entrance for about 0.2 mile to the parking lot just north of The Tarn. The trailhead is on the left (east) side of ME 3, across the road diagonally from the parking lot.

Key points:
0.0 Beachcroft Trailhead.
0.6 Reach the shoulder of Huguenot Head.
1.2 Arrive on the Champlain Mountain summit.
2.4 Return to the trailhead.

The hike: The Beachcroft Trail climbs to the shoulder of Huguenot Head, with an average elevation gain of 100 feet each tenth of a mile, but at times it feels remarkably

Beachcroft Trail
Bear Brook Trail

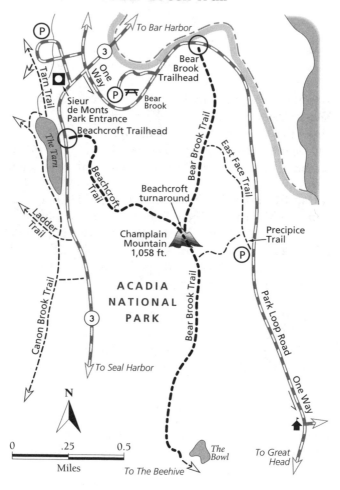

To Bar Harbor

Bear Brook Trailhead

One Way

Sieur de Monts Park Entrance

Bear Brook

Beachcroft Trailhead

Tarn Trail

The Tarn

Beachcroft Trail

Beachcroft turnaround

Bear Brook Trail

East Face Trail

Precipice Trail

Ladder Trail

Champlain Mountain 1,058 ft.

Canon Brook Trail

ACADIA NATIONAL PARK

Bear Brook Trail

Park Loop Road

One Way

To Seal Harbor

N

0   .25   0.5
Miles

The Bowl

To The Beehive

To Great Head

like a walk along a garden path. The gradual switchbacks and neatly laid stepping stones turn what would otherwise be a vertical scramble into a gentler ascent.

Adding to the wonder are the constant open views north toward Frenchman Bay, west toward Dorr Mountain, and east toward the summit of Champlain Mountain, the trail's goal.

The dome-shaped Huguenot Head, visible from Bar Harbor, has been a popular destination for more than a century. The Beachcroft Trail, built and rebuilt in the late 1800s and early 1900s, was named after the estate of the Bar Harbor summer resident who financed its construction. It consists of hundreds of hand-hewn stepping stones and countless switchbacks.

From the trailhead, ascend via the switchbacks and stone steps, catching your breath on the plentiful level sections along the way. Near the shoulder of Huguenot Head, the trail widens and levels off. It circles to the northeast at 0.6 mile, just below the head's summit.

The trail then dips into a gully before it begins the strenuous ascent up the steep west face of Champlain Mountain. The moderate part of the trail is over. Carefully pick your steps and follow the cairns up the rock face.

You will reach the open Champlain Mountain summit at 1.2 miles. Return the way you came.

Option: Climb to the shoulder of Huguenot Head for a shorter, easier hike of about 1.2 miles round-trip. You will still get most of the views.

4
BEAR BROOK TRAIL

see map page 18

Highlights: Enjoy expansive views from the summit of Champlain Mountain and all along the open ridge.

Type of hike: Out-and-back.

Total distance: 2.2 miles to the summit and back, or 5.2 miles to the trail's end and back.

Map: USGS Acadia National Park and Vicinity.

Parking and trailhead facilities: There is a mall parking area on the left (north), across the road just beyond the trailhead. No facilities are available.

Finding the trailhead: Enter the park at the Sieur de Monts entrance, which is about 2 miles south of downtown Bar Harbor on Maine 3. Turn right (south) on the one-way Park Loop Road. The trailhead is 0.8 mile from the entrance, on the right (south) after the Bear Brook picnic area.

Key points:
0.0 Bear Brook Trailhead.
0.4 Reach the junction with the East Face Trail.
1.1 Arrive at the Champlain Mountain summit, and the junction with the Precipice Trail.
2.6 Reach The Bowl.
5.2 Return to the trailhead.

The hike: We hiked the Bear Brook Trail early one morning, and saw a blanket of fog roll in to Frenchman Bay, enveloping the Porcupine Islands in the space of a few minutes. Amazingly, the ridgetop trail continued to be bathed in sunshine as the foghorns sounded their warnings below. Contrasts like these are possible only in Acadia, where the mountains meet the sea.

The Bear Brook Trail goes along the great ridge that, of all the park's ridges, is closest to the ocean. The trail offers spectacular views from Frenchman Bay to Great Head as it climbs Champlain Mountain, and then descends to the mountain pond known as The Bowl. It provides the most moderate access of all the trails up Champlain's summit.

From the trailhead, head south and start ascending through a birch grove and up a stone and log stairway. The sounds of a power plant can be heard almost all the way up to the summit.

The trail levels off a bit at about 0.2 mile, and then ascends more steeply up some stone steps. The junction with the East Face Trail is at 0.4 mile. Continue straight (south), and climb a steep pink granite face. Follow blue blazes as you near the summit.

The 1,058-foot summit of Champlain Mountain, at 1.1 miles, offers the closest mountaintop views of the Porcupine Islands in all of Acadia.

Many people turn around at the summit, for a round-trip hike of 2.2 miles. However, for the hardy hiker looking for more mileage and views, the Bear Brook Trail descends the ridge for another 1.5 miles, presenting views of Sand Beach, Great Head, The Beehive, The Bowl, and Gorham Mountain. Carefully follow the blue blazes. The trail ends at The Bowl at 2.6 miles.

Return the way you came, for a round trip of 5.2 miles.

Option: In late summer—after the peregrine falcon chicks that hatch every year along the cliffs of Champlain Mountain mature and fly off—you can do a strenuous loop by adding the East Face and Precipice Trails to the hike. While the loop adds on less than 0.5 mile to the total distance to the Champlain Mountain summit and back, it is very difficult, featuring a near-vertical ascent up the Precipice, with iron rungs for handholds and footholds. To add these trails to your hike, bear left (southeast) at the junction with the East Face Trail, which is 0.4 mile south of the Bear Brook Trailhead. Descend for about 0.5 mile along Champlain's rocky east face. At the junction with the Precipice Trail, bear right (southwest) and climb steeply for another 0.5 mile to the summit of Champlain. Return by turning right (north) and heading down the ridge back to the Bear Brook Trailhead.

5
JESUP PATH
(GREAT MEADOW LOOP)

Highlights: This woods and field walk takes you by the Great Meadow, Sieur de Monts Spring, the Wild Gardens of Acadia, the Nature Center, Abbe Museum, and The Tarn.
Type of hike: Out-and-back.
Total distance: 2 miles.
Map: USGS Acadia National Park and Vicinity.
Parking and trailhead facilities: There is a small gravel pullout at the trailhead on the right (south) side of the one-way Park Loop Road. No facilities are available.

Finding the trailhead: From the park's visitor center, drive south on the Park Loop Road for about 3 miles and turn left (east) at the sign for Sand Beach. Follow the one-way Park Loop Road for about 1.7 miles to the trailhead, which is on the right (south) soon after a road comes in on the left (north).

Key points:
0.0 Jesup Path Trailhead.
0.1 Pass through the Great Meadow.
0.3 At the junction with old gravel road, go straight (southeast).
0.7 At the junction with Stratheden Trail, go straight (south).
0.8 Reach the Sieur de Monts Spring area.

Jesup Path

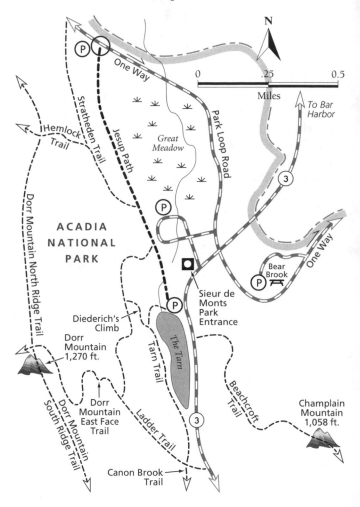

1.0 Arrive at The Tarn.
2.0 Return to the trailhead.

The hike: First created nearly 100 years ago as part of a garden path that connected to downtown Bar Harbor, Jesup Path leads from the Park Loop Road to the Sieur de Monts Spring area and the mountain pond known as The Tarn. As of fall 2000, through the efforts of Friends of Acadia, Jesup Path has been extended beyond the park's borders as part of the Great Meadow Loop, which reconnects Acadia to the outskirts of Bar Harbor.

From the trailhead, the well-graded path heads south, and skirts the Great Meadow at 0.1 mile. Views from this open marsh include Huguenot Head and Champlain Mountain to the left (southeast), and Dorr Mountain to the right (southwest).

A series of plank bridges takes you over the wet spots. Bring insect repellent during mosquito season. At about 0.3 mile, you'll come to a four-way intersection with an old road. Cross the road and go straight (southeast) across another plank bridge and into the woods. The trail then goes over a long series of log bridges.

At about 0.7 mile, you will come to the four-way junction with the Stratheden Trail. Cross over the old gravel road and continue straight (south).

At 0.8 mile, Jesup Path reaches the Sieur de Monts Spring area, which features the Wild Gardens of Acadia, the Nature Center, the Abbe Museum, and the spring itself. You can spend hours here learning about the flora and history of the park.

To continue on the trail, cross another plank bridge and reach The Tarn at 1 mile, in the gorge between Huguenot Head and Dorr Mountain. A plaque at this end of the trail reads, "In Memory of Morris K. and Maria DeWitt Jesup, Lovers of this Island, 1918."

Return the way you came, for a 2-mile round trip.

Options: For an easy loop of about 2.6 miles, follow Jesup Path as described above, but on the return from Sieur de Monts Spring, bear left at the first four-way intersection and follow the Stratheden Trail to the Park Loop Road. Turn right (east) on the loop road; you will arrive at your car after walking about 0.3 mile.

Trails outside the park are beyond the scope of this guide, but this new part of the trail can be picked up on Cromwell Harbor Road, south of Bar Harbor and west of Maine 3. For more information, contact the Friends of Acadia by calling (800) 625-0321 or by visiting their website at www.friendsofacadia.org.

GORHAM MOUNTAIN AREA

6
SAND BEACH AND GREAT HEAD TRAIL

Highlights: Enjoy Acadia's only ocean beach, made of sand, tiny shell fragments, and quartz pink feldspar, as well as grand views from Great Head.
Type of hike: Loop.
Total distance: 1.4 miles.
Map: USGS Acadia National Park and Vicinity.
Parking and trailhead facilities: The Sand Beach parking lot is on the left (east) side of the one-way Park Loop Road. Restrooms are open from late spring to early fall; there is also a changing area on the beach, and a pay phone.

Finding the trailhead: From the park's visitor center, drive south on the Park Loop Road for about 3 miles and turn left (east) at the sign for Sand Beach. Follow the one-way Park Loop Road for about 5.5 miles, past the park fee station, to the beach. The trailhead is down the stairs and on the far eastern end of the beach.

Sand Beach and Great Head Trail
Ocean Path

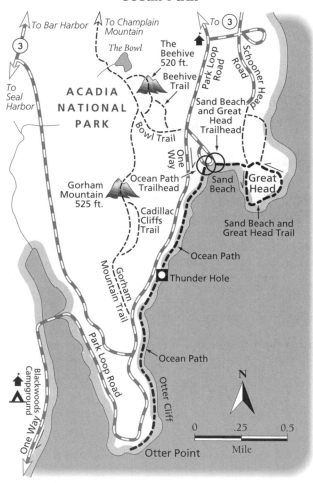

Key points:

0.0 Begin at the Great Head Trailhead, which is at the east end of Sand Beach.

0.1 Bear right (southeast) at the top of the stairs.

0.2 At the junction with the spur trail inland, go right (south) along the shore.

0.5 Reach the south end of the Great Head peninsula.

0.8 Arrive on the Great Head summit.

1.1 At the junction with the spur trail to Great Head ridge, bear left (southwest).

1.4 Return to the trailhead, completing the loop.

The hike: A hike on the Great Head peninsula is a perfect way to break up a lazy afternoon lounging on Sand Beach.

A relatively modest scramble up the rocky slope of Great Head leads you to spectacular views of the beach you just left behind, as well as views of The Beehive, Champlain Mountain, Otter Cliff, Egg Rock, and the Cranberry Isles. Also visible just off the tip of the peninsula is an unusual rock formation called Old Soaker.

The trail, built more than 150 years ago, was popular with artists and tourists beginning in the 1840s and 1850s. A teahouse once stood on Great Head, and the ruins of it are still visible. A large millstone near the trailhead is another reminder of man's history here.

Today, during the busy summer season, you may see boaters coming close to the Great Head cliffs, or rock climbers tackling the sheer face.

To get to the trailhead from the parking lot, head down the stairs to the beach and travel to the farthest (easternmost) end. Cross a channel—best at low tide to keep your feet dry—to the Great Head Trailhead.

Go up the series of 41 steps, bordered by a split rail fence. At the top of the steps at 0.1 mile, turn right (southeast), and follow the blue blazes up the rocky ledges. Views of Sand Beach, The Beehive, and Champlain Mountain are immediately visible. At the next trail junction at about 0.2 mile, bear right (south) to head toward the tip of the peninsula, with views of rectangular-shaped Old Soaker near by, and Otter Cliff and the Cranberry Isles in the distance.

At 0.5 mile, the trail rounds the peninsula. At 0.8 mile, it reaches the summit of Great Head, where there are views of Frenchman Bay and Egg Rock. At about 1.1 miles, along a level section of the trail, you will reach a junction in a birch grove. Turn left (southwest), and ascend gradually up Great Head ridge, with views of Champlain Mountain, The Beehive, and Gorham Mountain. At the last junction, bear right (northwest) to return to the trailhead and Sand Beach, for a loop hike of 1.4 miles.

Option: A longer loop, of about 1.7 miles, is possible by adding on a path through the woods. At the trail junction in the birch grove at 1.1 miles, head straight (northwest), instead of going left and up Great Head ridge. The trail comes out near the Schooner Head Road parking lot. Turn left (southwest) to continue on the woods trail for another 0.4 mile back to Sand Beach.

7
OCEAN PATH

see map page 28

Highlights: This hike takes you to Thunder Hole, Otter Cliff, and along the pink granite shoreline.

Type of hike: Out-and-back.

Total distance: 4 miles.

Map: USGS Acadia National Park and Vicinity.

Parking and trailhead facilities: Sand Beach parking lot is on the left (east) side of the one-way Park Loop Road. Restrooms are open from spring to early fall; there is a changing area on the beach, and a pay phone.

Finding the trailhead: From the park's visitor center, drive south on the Park Loop Road for about 3 miles and turn left (east) at the sign for Sand Beach. Follow the one-way Park Loop Road for about 5.5 miles, past the park fee station, to the beach. The trailhead is on the right (east) just before the stairs to the beach.

Key points:
0.0 Ocean Path Trailhead.
1.0 Reach Thunder Hole.
1.3 Pass the Gorham Mountain Trailhead, which is across the Park Loop Road.
1.8 Reach Otter Cliff.
2.0 Arrive at Otter Point.
4.0 Return to the trailhead.

The hike: The sounds of the ocean and the views of rocky cliffs and pink granite shoreline are never far from Ocean Path. At Thunder Hole, halfway along the path, when the conditions are just right, the surf crashes through rocky chasms with a thunderous roar. And at Otter Point, at trail's end, the sound of a buoy ringing fills the air. Rock climbers can be seen scaling Otter Cliff, one of the premier rock climbing areas in the eastern United States, while picnickers and sun worshippers can be found enjoying themselves on the flat pink granite slabs that dot the shore here.

First used as a buckboard road in the 1870s, Ocean Path and Ocean Drive were rebuilt in the 1930s by the Civilian Conservation Corps, with funding assistance from John D. Rockefeller Jr. Because of its ease and accessibility, Ocean Path can be crowded during the height of the tourist season. The best time to walk it is either very early or very late on a summer's day, or in the spring or fall as we have.

Ocean Path Trailhead is on the right just before the stairs to Sand Beach. Follow the gravel path past the changing rooms and restrooms, up a series of stairs, then left (south) from a secondary parking area. The very easy trail takes you southwest along the shore, paralleling the Ocean Drive section of the Park Loop Road.

Thunder Hole, a popular destination, is at 1 mile. Many visitors driving through the park on calm summer days stop here and cause a traffic jam, but go away disappointed. It turns out the best time to experience the power of Thunder Hole is right after a storm, when the surf crashes violently through the chasm, pushing trapped air against the rock and creating a reverberating boom.

At 1.3 miles, you will pass a short series of stairs on the right (west), which lead you across the Park Loop Road to the Gorham Mountain Trailhead. All along the route, the pink granite shoreline attracts picnickers and bird watchers.

The path's only noticeable elevation gain comes as it rises through the woods toward Otter Cliff, reached at 1.8 miles. On the approach, rock climbers can be seen scaling the rock face or waiting at the top of the cliff for their turn. A staircase leads down on the left (east) to the rock climber's registration board.

The path ends at 2 miles, at Otter Point, where there is a parking lot. Return the way you came for a 4-mile round trip.

Options: To make this an easy shuttle hike, leave one car at Sand Beach parking lot, and drive to Otter Point to hike the trail 2 miles one way back to Sand Beach.

Or make a moderate 3.4-mile loop by adding on the Gorham Mountain and Bowl Trails. At the trail junction 1.3 miles from the Ocean Path Trailhead, take the stairs leading across the Park Loop Road to the Gorham Mountain Trailhead. Head north on the Gorham Mountain Trail for 1.5 miles, then turn right and head east on the Bowl Trail for 0.6 mile, back to the Sand Beach parking lot. See Hike 9 for more details.

Or, when the free Island Explorer bus shuttle is operating, from late June through Labor Day, leave a car at Otter Point, hike one way to Thunder Hole or Sand Beach, and catch the shuttle back to the car.

The Bowl Trail
Gorham Mountain Trail

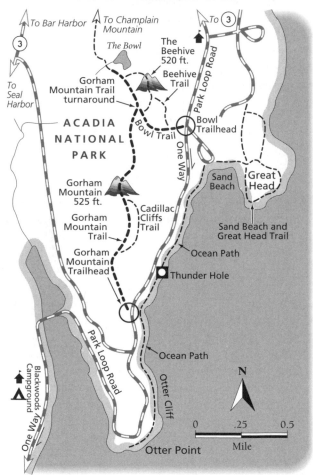

To Bar Harbor
To Champlain Mountain
To (3)
The Bowl
The Beehive 520 ft.
Gorham Mountain Trail turnaround
Beehive Trail
Bowl Trailhead
ACADIA NATIONAL PARK
Bowl Trail
One Way
Sand Beach
Great Head
Gorham Mountain 525 ft.
Gorham Mountain Trail
Cadillac Cliffs Trail
Sand Beach and Great Head Trail
Gorham Mountain Trailhead
Ocean Path
Thunder Hole
To Seal Harbor
(3)
Park Loop Road
Ocean Path
Blackwoods Campground
One Way
Park Loop Road
Otter Cliff
Otter Point
N
0   .25   0.5
Mile

8
THE BOWL TRAIL

Highlights: This hike leads to a mountain pond nestled behind The Beehive.
Type of hike: Out-and-back.
Total distance: 1.6 miles.
Map: USGS Acadia National Park and Vicinity.
Parking and trailhead facilities: The Sand Beach parking lot is on the left (east) side of the one-way Park Loop Road. Restrooms are open in the summer. There is also a changing area on the beach, and a pay phone.

Finding the trailhead: From the park's visitor center, drive south on the Park Loop Road for about 3 miles and turn left (east) at the sign for Sand Beach. Follow the one-way Park Loop Road for about 5.5 miles, past the park fee station, to the beach. The trailhead is across the Park Loop Road from the beach.

Key points:
0.0 The Bowl Trailhead.
0.2 Reach the junction with the Beehive Trail.
0.4 Meet the junction with the spur trail to the Gorham Mountain Trail.
0.5 Arrive at the junction with spur trail to The Beehive.
0.6 Reach the junction with the Gorham Mountain Trail.
0.8 Arrive at The Bowl.
1.6 Return to the trailhead.

The hike: Views of a great blue heron taking off low across the water's surface, or of a turkey vulture soaring high on the thermals, are among the possible rewards when you hike to The Bowl, a mountain pond at more than 400 feet in elevation.

We got lucky and got both views in the same day as we hiked along the section of the trail that skirts the shoreline. Hike in the early morning or late afternoon to improve your chances of such sightings.

The Bowl Trail climbs gradually, passing junctions with the Beehive Trailhead at 0.2 mile, a spur to the Gorham Mountain Trail at 0.4 mile, another spur to The Beehive at 0.5 mile, and the Gorham Mountain Trail at 0.6 mile.

Beyond, the Bowl Trail heads up steeply through the woods, then goes downhill, arriving at The Bowl at the 0.8-mile mark.

Return the way you came.

Options: If you are not afraid of heights, you can do a loop by first going up the 0.8-mile Beehive Trail, then down the Bowl Trail. Once at The Bowl, turn left (southwest) along the pond's shore, and take the Bowl Trail back to your car.

Or add about 1.2 miles round-trip for spectacular views from 525-foot Gorham Mountain. After hiking 0.4 mile from the Bowl Trailhead, turn left (south) at the short spur to the Gorham Mountain Trail, and bear left again until the summit is reached in 0.6 mile.

Return the way you came.

9
GORHAM MOUNTAIN TRAIL

see map page 34

Highlights: This hike features views of Great Head, Sand Beach, Otter Cliff, Champlain Mountain, and The Beehive, as well as a spur trail to Cadillac Cliffs and an ancient sea cave.

Type of hike: Out-and-back.

Total distance: 3 miles.

Map: USGS Acadia National Park and Vicinity.

Parking and trailhead facilities: The Gorham Mountain parking lot on the right (west) side of the one-way Park Loop Road. There are no facilities.

Finding the trailhead: From the park's visitor center, drive south on the Park Loop Road for about 3 miles, and turn left (east) at the sign for Sand Beach. Follow the one-way Park Loop Road for about 7 miles, passing the park fee station, Sand Beach, and Thunder Hole, to the Gorham Mountain sign.

Key points:

0.0 Gorham Mountain Trailhead.

0.2 Reach the junction with the southern end of the Cadillac Cliffs Trail.

0.5 Pass the junction with the northern end of the Cadillac Cliffs Trail.

0.9 Arrive on the Gorham Mountain summit.

1.4 Pass the junction with the spur trail to the Bowl Trail.
1.5 The trail ends at the Bowl Trail.
3.0 Return to the trailhead.

The hike: The Gorham Mountain Trail provides some of the most rewarding views in Acadia for relatively modest effort, featuring nearly uninterrupted ridge-top panoramas of everything from Great Head and Sand Beach to The Beehive. The trail follows the great ridge that runs north all the way to Champlain Mountain, and is closest to the ocean of all of Acadia's mountain ridges.

An additional bonus, if you choose to take it, is the 0.5-mile spur trail to the once-submerged Cadillac Cliffs and an ancient sea cave, which illustrates the powerful geologic forces that helped shape Mount Desert Island.

From the Gorham Mountain parking lot, climb gradually up open ledges, heading north. At 0.2 mile, the Cadillac Cliffs Trail leads right (northeast), paralleling and then rejoining the Gorham Mountain Trail at 0.5 mile. If you're inclined to add the Cadillac Cliffs spur, it is best to do it on the ascent rather than the descent, because of the iron rungs and steep rock face along the way.

Continue on the Gorham Mountain Trail as it moderately ascends the ridge. Pass the junction with the northern end of the Cadillac Cliffs Trail at 0.5 mile. All along this portion of the route you will enjoy views south to Otter Cliff, east to Great Head and Sand Beach, and north to The Beehive and Champlain Mountain. Visible in the distance at various points are Frenchman Bay and Egg Rock.

The summit of Gorham Mountain, at 525 feet, is at 0.9 mile. Though many hikers turn around here, the trail continues north down the ridge, passing the junction with a spur to the Bowl Trail at 1.4 miles, and ending officially at the Bowl Trail at 1.5 miles.

Return the way you came, adding on the Cadillac Cliffs Trail if you choose.

Option: For a 3.4-mile loop that includes the Ocean Path, take Gorham Mountain Trail to its end at the Bowl Trail. Turn right (southeast) on the Bowl Trail, and travel 0.6 mile toward the Park Loop Road and Sand Beach. Cross the road and the Sand Beach parking lot to the Ocean Path Trailhead, which is on the right just before the stairs to the beach (see Hike 7). Follow the path past the changing rooms and restrooms, up a series of stairs, then left (south), when you reach a secondary parking area. Follow the very easy gravel path that parallels the ocean and the Park Loop Road, reaching the Gorham Mountain Trailhead parking lot in 1.3 miles.

Jordan Pond Nature Trail
Jordan Pond Shore Trail

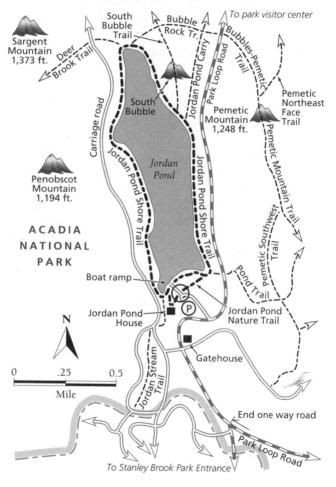

Sargent Mountain 1,373 ft.

South Bubble Trail

Bubble Rock Tr.

To park visitor center

Deer Brook Trail

Bubbles-Pemetic Trail

Pemetic Northeast Face Trail

South Bubble

Jordan Pond Carry

Park Loop Road

Pemetic Mountain 1,248 ft.

Carriage road

Jordan Pond Shore Trail

Jordan Pond

Penobscot Mountain 1,194 ft.

ACADIA NATIONAL PARK

Jordan Pond Shore Trail

Pemetic Mountain Trail

Pemetic Southwest Trail

Boat ramp

Pond Trail

Jordan Pond House

Jordan Pond Nature Trail

P

Gatehouse

N

0   .25   0.5
Mile

Jordan Stream Trail

End one way road

To Stanley Brook Park Entrance

Park Loop Road

JORDAN POND, BUBBLES, AND EAGLE LAKE AREA

10
JORDAN POND
NATURE TRAIL

Highlights: This interpretive nature trail leads through woods and along Jordan Pond.
Type of hike: Loop.
Total distance: 0.5 mile.
Map: USGS Acadia National Park and Vicinity.
Parking and trailhead facilities: Park at the Jordan Pond parking lot, where there is a chemical toilet. The restaurant, gift shop, and restrooms are open from late spring to early summer at the nearby Jordan Pond House.

Finding the trailhead: From the park's visitor center, head south on the two-way Park Loop Road for about 7.6 miles and turn right (north) into the Jordan Pond parking lot (not the Jordan Pond House parking lot). Park in the parking lot on the right. The trailhead is at the far end of the lot, at the top of the boat ramp road and on the right (northeast).

Key points:

0.0 Jordan Pond Nature Trailhead.

0.2 Bear left (west), after trail post 3, at the shore of Jordan Pond and the junction with the Jordan Pond Shore Trail.

0.3 Cross the foot of the boat ramp after trail post 7.

0.4 Bear left twice, at the fork after post 8, and after post 9.

0.5 Return to the trailhead, completing the loop.

The hike: A lot is packed into this short interpretive trail: Panoramic views of Jordan Pond and the distinctive Bubbles on its far shore, and lessons in history and nature. But, because it is so accessible, be prepared for the trail to be packed with people during the height of the summer season.

The trail begins in the woods, heading right (northeast) at the top of the boat ramp road. A descriptive brochure is available for purchase for 50 cents, or you can borrow one from the box provided and return it at trail's end.

The first two numbered trail posts take you through deep forests of balsam fir and red spruce, then under broad-leafed American beeches and towering northern white cedars.

At 0.2 mile and trail post 3, a short spur along a stone walk on the right leads you to the edge of a wetland. The main trail then brings you to the shores of Jordan Pond and a junction with the Jordan Pond Shore Trail. Go left (west) on the nature trail.

At post 5, you get a grand view of the distinctive twin mountains known as The Bubbles on the far shore. And at post 6, you get a lesson in the geology and history of Acadia, with the brochure describing the distinctive granite found here, and the dramatic scenery that has attracted artists since the 1840s.

Cross the foot of the boat ramp after post 7 at 0.3 mile. At post 8, a plaque describes the power of glaciers in shaping Acadia. Then, at 0.4 mile, bear left at a fork back into the woods to post 9. Here, the brochure describes how the Jordan Pond House tradition of afternoon tea and popovers came into being around 1900. Bear left at post 9 to circle back to the parking lot.

Option: If the walk has gotten you hungry for some of Jordan Pond House's famous popovers, bear right at post 9 for a short stroll to the restaurant.

11
JORDAN POND SHORE TRAIL

see map page 40

Highlights: On this hike, you will have expansive views of Jordan Pond, The Bubbles and Jordan Cliffs, as well as a chance to glimpse a colorful merganser duck.

Type of hike: Loop.

Total distance: 3.3 miles.

Map: USGS Acadia National Park and Vicinity.

Parking and trailhead facilities: Park in the Jordan Pond parking lot. The restaurant, gift shop, and restrooms are at the nearby Jordan Pond House, and are open in summer.

Finding the trailhead: From the park's visitor center, head south on the Park Loop Road for about 7.6 miles and turn right (north) into the Jordan Pond parking lot (not the Jordan Pond House parking lot). Park at the parking lot on the right. Follow the boat ramp road to the shore of the pond. The trailhead is on the right (east).

Key points:

0.0 Jordan Pond Shore Trailhead.

0.1 Reach the junction with Jordan Pond Nature Trail.

1.0 Pass the junction with Jordan Pond Carry Trail.

1.1 Reach the junction with South Bubble Trail.

1.5 Pass the junction with Bubble Rock Trail.

1.6 Pass the junction with Deer Brook Trail.

3.2 Arrive at Jordan Pond House.

The hike: A vigorous walk around Jordan Pond, capped by afternoon tea and popovers on the lawn of the Jordan Pond House—it's one of those special Acadia experiences.

The trail starts from the boat ramp at the Jordan Pond parking lot, and immediately offers a spectacular view of the distinctive rounded mountains known as The Bubbles, which lie north across the pond. Bear right (east), circling the pond counterclockwise.

The first half of the trail is along the easy eastern shore, but be prepared for the western shore's jagged rocks and exposed roots. Wear proper footwear.

At 0.1 mile, you will reach the first of several trails that diverge from the Jordan Pond Shore Trail. Bear left, paralleling the shore at each of the junctions. The trail rounds the bend at the south end of the pond and begins heading north. You will soon start seeing Jordan Cliffs to the west, across the pond. There are plenty of boulders along the shore to sit on and admire the crystal clear waters and the tremendous views. Jordan Pond serves as a public water supply, so no swimming is allowed.

After passing over a series of wood bridges, you will soon come up under the towering pinkish granite of South Bubble. At a small coarse-sand beach, a log bench allows you to take in the long view back south across the pond, to the Jordan Pond House. Cross another wooden bridge; at 1 mile you will reach the Jordan Pond Carry Trail, which veers to the right (north) and leads 1 mile to Eagle Lake.

At 1.1 miles, the South Bubble Trail goes up (right/north) for 0.4 mile to the summit of South Bubble and the precariously perched Bubble Rock. The trail now gets more difficult, ascending a bit above the shoreline and crossing a boulder-strewn section. Birches and cedars dominate the woods here. At 1.5 miles, pass the junction with the Bubble Rock Trail, which heads right (east) up the gap between North and South Bubbles. Look back toward South Bubble, and you will get a good view of Bubble Rock.

You are now at the northernmost end of the pond and can get good views of the Jordan Pond House to the south and The Bubbles to the east. Cross a series of intricate wood bridges—one has an archway in the middle.

At 1.6 miles, pass the junction with the Deer Brook Trail, which leads up toward Jordan Cliffs. Now begins the trail's traverse of the rough western shore of the pond, with its rocks and roots, ups and downs. After a bit of hide-and-seek with the shore and a long stretch of rock hopping, you will reach a series of wooden bridges and a long boardwalk that takes you over creeks and fragile marshland. In addition to the dramatic views of The Bubbles, you may also catch a glimpse of a blue jay or a common merganser, as we did. It is hard to miss a merganser, especially a female, with its distinctive rust-colored, crested head, and orange bill.

At 3.2 miles, pass near the Jordan Pond House, where you can stop for afternoon tea and popovers on the expansive lawn, with a grand view of The Bubbles as backdrop. At 3.3 miles, the trail ends back at the Jordan Pond parking lot.

Options: Walk just the easier eastern shore to the junction at 1 mile with the Jordan Pond Carry Trail, and return the way you came for a 2-mile round trip. Or, add the short but steep trip up the South Bubble Trail, tagging on an extra 0.8 mile to the summit and back.

You can also loop around Jordan Pond but skip the rocky western shore, by taking the Deer Brook Trail up to the carriage road. Turn left (south) on the carriage road and walk about 1.5 miles to the Jordan Pond House. From the Jordan Pond House, follow a woods path back to the Jordan Pond parking lot.

Bubble Rock Trail

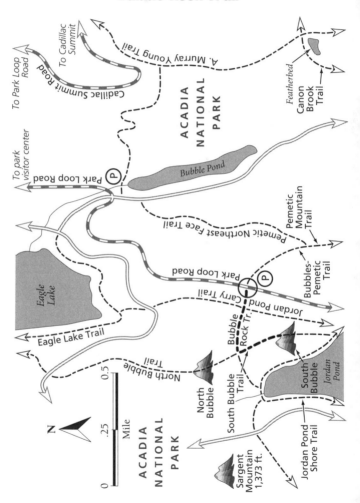

12
BUBBLE ROCK TRAIL

Highlights: This hike features 360-degree views from South Bubble, and a view of Bubble Rock.
Type of hike: Out-and-back.
Total distance: 1 mile.
Map: USGS Acadia National Park and Vicinity.
Parking and trailhead facilities: The Bubble Rock parking lot is on the right (west) side, of the Park Loop Road. There are no facilities.

Finding the trailhead: From the park's visitor center, drive south on the Park Loop Road for about 6 miles, past the Cadillac Mountain entrance and the Bubble Pond parking lot, to the Bubble Rock parking lot. The trailhead departs from the Bubble Rock parking lot.

Key points:
0.0 Bubble Rock Trailhead.
0.1 Reach the junction with the Jordan Pond Carry Trail.
0.3 At the junction with the South Bubble and North Bubble trails, turn left (south).
0.5 Reach the South Bubble summit and Bubble Rock.
1.0 Return to the trailhead.

The hike: By going up into the gap between South and North Bubbles, this trail provides the shortest route up either of the distinctive rounded mountains that overlook Jordan Pond. The trip also takes you to Bubble Rock, precariously perched on the summit of South Bubble, high above the Park Loop Road.

Heading west from the Bubble Rock parking lot, the trail crosses the Jordan Pond Carry Trail at 0.1 mile. At the junction with the South Bubble and North Bubble trails at 0.3 mile, turn left (south) to the South Bubble. Reach the 768-foot summit at 0.5 mile. A sign points to nearby Bubble Rock.

Return the way you came.

Option: You can reach the North Bubble by adding on a walk of 0.8-mile round trip. Hike down from South Bubble, and instead of turning right (east) through the gap to head back to the parking area, go straight (north), reaching the North Bubble after 0.4 mile. Return the way you came.

13
EAGLE LAKE TRAIL

Highlights: Hike along the second largest lake in Acadia, and obtain access to the little-traveled Conners Nubble, a low mountain north of The Bubbles.

Type of hike: Out-and-back.

Total distance: 3.6 miles, plus 0.4 mile round-trip to the trailhead and back.

Map: USGS Acadia National Park and Vicinity.

Parking and trailhead facilities: Park at Bubble Pond parking lot, where there is a chemical toilet and a picnic table.

Finding the trailhead: From the park visitor center, head south on the Park Loop Road for about 5 miles, past the Cadillac Mountain entrance, to the Bubble Pond parking lot (not the Bubble Rock parking lot, which is farther south). Cross to the other side of the Park Loop Road and follow the carriage road for about 0.2 mile to carriage road intersection 7. Bear left (west). Eagle Lake Trailhead is on the right, along southeast shore of Eagle Lake.

Key points:

0.0 Begin at the Eagle Lake Trailhead, which is 0.2 mile along the carriage road from the parking lot.

0.6 Pass the junction with the Jordan Pond Carry Trail.

1.7 Reach the North Bubble Trail, and the intersection with the 0.4-mile spur trail to Conners Nubble.

Eagle Lake Trail

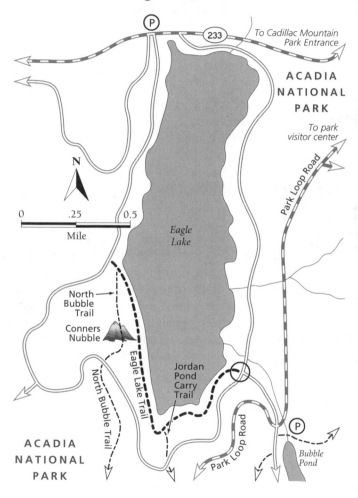

1.8 Arrive at the carriage road.
3.6 Return to the trailhead.

The hike: Like other lake and pond hikes in Acadia, the Eagle Lake Trail can be walked just for its water views, or for the access it provides to nearby mountains. What we feel is particularly special about this trail is the access it provides to the lesser-known Conners Nubble, just north of the highly popular Bubbles. And, like similar trails, the Eagle Lake Trail has its easy, flat sections and its rougher up-and-down sections.

The trail begins by following the easy east shore, and heads west to the rougher side. Dense cedars line the start of the trail. A long series of log bridges takes you over the wettest part of the path.

At 0.6 mile, you will reach a junction with the Jordan Carry Trail, part of which was once used by Native Americans to carry canoes from one body of water to another. This junction marks the start of the west shore of Eagle Lake.

The trail heads in and out of the woods and goes by a sandy beach; no swimming is allowed here. Cross a field of rocks at about 0.8 mile. Stay straight here rather than bearing left into the woods, which so many others have mistakenly done that a worn-down, wrong-way path has been created. The path gets rockier and more difficult as you skirt the western shore. You will cross the base of a rockslide. A final little uphill brings you inland into a birch grove; the trail levels off into a woods path once again.

At 1.7 miles, reach a junction with the North Bubble Trail, which heads south to Conners Nubble and the North Bubble summit. The trail ends at 1.8 miles at a carriage road.

Return the way you came.

Options: To reach the open summit of Conners Nubble, turn left (south) and continue on the North Bubble Trail for 0.4 mile. Return the way you came.

To do a long loop up The Bubbles, turn left (south) on the North Bubble Trail, and take it up and over Conners Nubble, the North Bubble, and the South Bubble. Descend to the shore of Jordan Pond, and turn left (southeast) along the Jordan Pond Shore Trail. Take your next left and head northwest on the Jordan Pond Carry Trail, looping back to Eagle Lake. Turn right (northeast) on the Eagle Lake Trail, and return to the Bubble Pond parking area. The loop is approximately 5.4 miles.

14
DAY MOUNTAIN TRAIL

Highlights: This trail offers the closest mountain views of the Cranberry Isles, as well as the hidden Champlain Monument. Watch for horse-drawn carriages and bicyclists at the carriage road crossings.

Type of hike: Out-and-back.

Total distance: 2.6 miles.

Map: USGS Acadia National Park and Vicinity.

Parking and trailhead facilities: Park in the gravel pullout along the Park Loop Road just before the Day Mountain carriage road overpass.

Finding the trailhead: From the Sieur de Monts entrance to the park, head south on the one-way Park Loop Road for about 8 miles. Go under the Maine 3 overpass to the next overpass, where the Day Mountain carriage road goes over the Park Loop Road on a stone bridge. Look for a wooden sign that says "Path to Carriage Road," which is on the right (north) side just before the carriage road overpass. Take the path up, turn left (south), and cross the Day Mountain carriage road bridge to the trailhead.

Key points:

0.0 Day Mountain Trailhead.

0.4 Cross the carriage road.

0.5 Reach the Day Mountain summit.

Day Mountain Trail

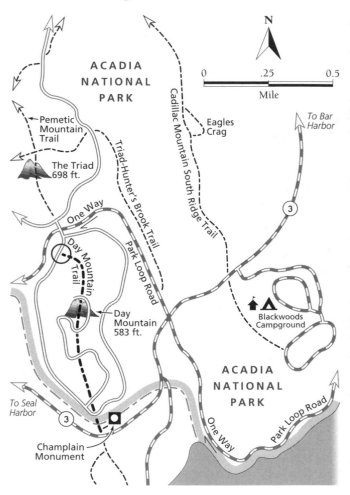

N

0   .25   0.5
Mile

ACADIA
NATIONAL
PARK

Pemetic
Mountain
Trail

The Triad
698 ft.

Cadillac Mountain South Ridge Trail

Eagles
Crag

To Bar
Harbor

One Way

Triad-Hunter's Brook Trail

Day
Mountain
Trail

Day
Mountain
583 ft.

Park Loop Road

3

Blackwoods
Campground

To Seal
Harbor

3

Champlain
Monument

ACADIA
NATIONAL
PARK

One Way

Park Loop Road

0.6 Cross the carriage road again.

0.7 Bear left just before the carriage road, then cross over at the cairn.

1.0 Cross the carriage road.

1.1 Bear right on the carriage road to carriage road intersection 36 before crossing over.

1.3 Reach ME 3, turn left (east) to Champlain Monument.

2.6 Return to the trailhead.

The hike: Good things come in small packages, as this little hike proves. Day Mountain is only 583 feet in elevation and a mere 0.5 mile from the trailhead, but it provides close-up views of the Cranberry Isles to the south, and you can see spectacular sunsets to the west, as we did when we hiked this close to dusk. The hike provides a little gem at trail's end—a hidden monument to the French explorer Samuel de Champlain, who gave Mount Desert Island its name.

Heading south from the trailhead, the Day Mountain Trail rises swiftly through the woods and crosses a carriage road at 0.4 mile. The trail attains the Day Mountain summit at 0.5 mile, with its views of the Cranberry Isles to the south and Gorham Mountain to the northeast. You can turn around here if you just came for the sunset, or you can continue south toward ME 3 and the Champlain Monument.

To continue, cross the only carriage road that gradually winds up Day Mountain at 0.6 mile—the first of four road crossings you will make on the way down. You may see bicyclists and horse-drawn carriages from the nearby Wildwood Stables along this popular carriage road, so look both ways before crossing.

At 0.7 mile, bear left (east) and follow the cairns just before you come upon the carriage road again. Cross over at the final cairn. Some of the best views on the trail are visible along this part of the carriage road, looking toward Otter Point to the east, the Cranberry Isles to the south, and Somes Sound to the west.

Descend steeply at times. At 1 mile, cross the carriage road again. Then, at 1.1 miles, bear right on the carriage road to intersection 36 before crossing to the other side of the road for the fourth and final time.

At 1.3 miles, bear left (east) at the sign pointing to Champlain Monument, just before ME 3. The granite monument, hidden in the woods, says, "In honor of Samuel de Champlain. Born in France 1567. Died at Quebec 1635. A soldier, sailor, explorer and administrator who gave this island its name." Return the way you came.

Option: To loop back on the carriage road on the return from the Champlain Monument, turn right (northeast) at the first junction with the carriage road. Take the road about 1.5 miles back to the stone carriage road bridge by the Day Mountain Trailhead, and return to the parking area along the Park Loop Road.

Mount Desert Island West of Somes Sound

This is the quieter side of the island.

The major "best easy" Acadia National Park trails on the west side of Mount Desert Island go up or around such landmarks as Acadia and Flying Mountains, Beech Mountain, Beech Cliff, and Ship Harbor.

The most popular routes in the western mountains of the park are the Acadia and Flying Mountain trails, which offer close-up views of Somes Sound, the only fjord on the east coast of the United States; the trail up Beech Mountain to its fire tower; and the path to Beech Cliff, with its views down to Echo Lake.

The popular and easy Ship Harbor and Wonderland Trails are near Bass Harbor. Both of them go along the rocky pink granite shore that makes Acadia unique.

Acadia Mountain Trail
Flying Mountain Trail

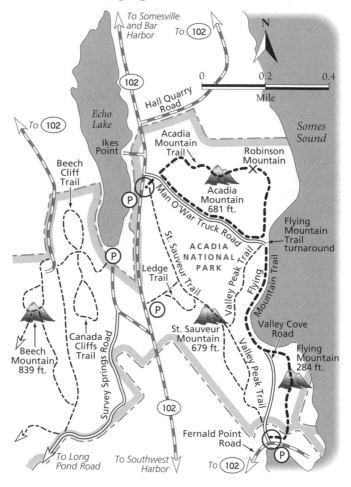

WESTERN MOUNTAINS AREA

15
ACADIA MOUNTAIN TRAIL

Highlights: Enjoy views of Somes Sound, Echo Lake, the Gulf of Maine, the Cranberry Isles, and the surrounding mountains from this trail.
Type of hike: Loop.
Total distance: 2.8 miles.
Map: USGS Acadia National Park and Vicinity.
Parking and trailhead facilities: Acadia Mountain parking lot is on the right (west) side of Maine 102. A chemical toilet is available.

Finding the trailhead: From Somesville, head south on Maine 102 for about 3 miles, past Ikes Point, to the Acadia Mountain parking lot. The trailhead is on the left, (east) side of ME 102.

Key points:
0.0 Acadia Mountain Trailhead.
0.1 At the St. Sauveur Trail junction, bear left (north).
0.2 Cross the gravel Man O' War Truck Road.

0.8 Reach the Acadia Mountain summit.

1.1 Arrive at Robinson Mountain.

1.7 At the junction with the spur to Man O' War Truck Road and the spur trail to Man O' War Brook, turn left (east) to the brook.

1.8 Reach Man O' War Brook.

1.9 Return to the junction with the spur trail to Man O' War Truck Road, and head straight (northwest) on the road.

2.6 At the junction, turn left (south) into woods.

2.7 Bear right (west) at the St. Sauveur Trail junction.

2.8 Return to ME 102 and the parking lot.

The hike: One of Acadia's more popular trails on the west side of Somes Sound, the Acadia Mountain Trail is a tough scramble up to spectacular views of Somes Sound, the ocean, and surrounding mountains. But as strenuous as it is, you may see families with small children making the trek.

At the junction with the St. Sauveur Trail at 0.1 mile, bear left (north) toward Acadia Mountain. At 0.2 mile, cross the gravel Man O' War Truck Road and continue on the Acadia Mountain Trail.

Now, the rough climb begins. At times, you need to pull yourself up 20-foot rock crevices. While the trail is largely well marked with cairns, there is a sharp left that is easy to miss.

The trail continues to steadily climb through forest, then takes you up a rocky section with switchbacks. You may hear the sounds of boats on Somes Sound, and you will soon get good views of the fjord.

Resume the steep ascent up the rock face via switch-backs. You will see Echo Lake for the first time behind you, to the west. The trail levels off a bit as you reach the 681-foot summit of Acadia Mountain at 0.8 mile. Here, from a rock promontory, you get expansive views of Somes Sound, as well as of Somesville to the north, and the Gulf of Maine and Cranberry Isles to the south. There is also a hidden trail that leads to the right, providing great views of Northeast Harbor and Southwest Harbor. You may choose to turn around here, although there are even better and more close-up views of the sound farther on.

The trail next takes you steeply down over jagged rock. At 1.1 miles, you come to a gorgeous view—perhaps one of the best on the island—atop a broad open summit. While there is no sign naming this peak, the USGS map shows this as Robinson Mountain. From here, you can see Beech Mountain with its fire tower to the west, Valley Cove and the Gulf of Maine to the south, as well as Somes Sound and Norumbega Mountain to the east.

The trail descends steeply from Robinson Mountain. At 1.7 miles, reach a junction with a spur trail to Man O' War Truck Road and a spur trail to Man O' War Brook. Turn left (southeast) at 1.8 miles to get a view of the brook cascading down into Somes Sound.

Return to the junction with the spur to the Man O' War Truck Road, following the gravel road northwest back to where the Acadia Mountain Trail crosses it, at 2.6 miles. Turn left (south) into the woods onto the Acadia Mountain Trail, then right (west) at the junction with the St. Sauveur Trail at 2.7 miles, returning to the Acadia

Mountain parking lot at 2.8 miles. Alternatively, you can take the Man O' War Truck Road until it ends at ME 102, then go left (south) on ME 102 back to the Acadia Mountain parking lot.

Option: For a rigorous loop of about 5.5 miles, do not head back to the Acadia Mountain Trailhead on the Man O' War Truck Road. Instead, follow the sign at the junction that is close to Man O' War Brook, hiking toward Flying Mountain. The 1.6-mile long Flying Mountain Trail takes you south along the rocky shore of Somes Sound and Valley Cove, then over Flying Mountain, with its great views of Fernald Point and the narrows at the mouth of the sound, and down to a parking area.

Cross the parking area, turn right (north) for 0.1 mile on the gravel Valley Cove Road, and then go left (northwest) on to the Valley Peak Trail. Follow the Valley Peak Trail northwest for 0.4 mile to Valley Peak. Continue northwest, taking the left fork toward the wooded summit of St. Sauveur Mountain. Stay straight on the 1.6-mile long St. Sauveur Trail along the mountain ridge, until it descends to the junction with the Acadia Mountain Trail. Turn left (west) to return to the Acadia Mountain parking area.

Note: The Valley Cove section of the Flying Mountain Trail may be closed during peregrine falcon season, from spring to late summer, as it was for the first time in 2000. If the closure occurs, this long loop is impossible to do. Check with park officials before attempting this option.

16
FLYING MOUNTAIN TRAIL

see map page 60

Highlights: This hike features views of Somes Sound, Fernald Cove, and the Cranberry Isles. The section of trail near Valley Cove may be closed during peregrine falcon breeding season, from spring through late summer.
Type of hike: Out-and-back.
Total distance: 3.2 miles.
Map: USGS Acadia National Park and Vicinity.
Parking and trailhead facilities: There is a small parking area on Fernald Point Road at the foot of Valley Cove Road. There are no facilities.

Finding the trailhead: From Somesville, head south on Maine 102 for about 4.5 miles, past the St. Sauveur Mountain parking lot. Turn left (east) onto Fernald Point Road, and travel about 1 mile to the parking area at the foot of the gravel Valley Cove Road. The trailhead is on the right (east) side of the parking area.

Key points:
0.0 Flying Mountain Trailhead.
0.3 Arrive on Flying Mountain.
0.7 Reach the junction with Valley Cove Road.
0.9 Arrive at Valley Cove.

1.6 Reach the junction with the trails to Acadia and St. Sauveur Mountains, Valley Peak, and Man O' War Truck Road.

3.2 Return to the trailhead.

The hike: Flying Mountain is one of the lowest peaks in Acadia, yet it offers some of the best views. It can be climbed as part of a short out-and-back scramble of as little as 0.6-mile round trip, or as part of a longer loop of up to 4.6 miles.

The trail ascends swiftly from the parking area, first through deep woods, and then up rocky ledges. At one point, the ledges serve as stone steps. Once you are above tree line and at the top of the rock face, you will get views to the southeast of Greening Island and the Cranberry Isles. To the northwest are the rocky cliffs of Valley Peak.

Dominating the view from the 284-foot Flying Mountain summit, at 0.3 mile, is the sandy peninsula known as Fernald Point. Across the Narrows at the mouth of Somes Sound is the town of Northeast Harbor, and in the distance are Greening Island and the Cranberry Isles. From here, you can see kayakers rounding Fernald Point and boaters entering and leaving Somes Sound. You can even hear a ferry blow its whistle in Northeast Harbor, as we did on one of our climbs here.

Some hikers turn around here, content with the views on Flying Mountain. But those who go on will be rewarded with scenes of Somes Sound and views of Norumbega, Penobscot, Sargent, and other mountains of Acadia. They will also be challenged by the ups and downs of the trail along the rough, rocky shores of Valley Cove.

Just beyond the summit of Flying Mountain, at 0.4 mile, you will get the first glimpse of the northern reaches of Somes Sound, as well as of Acadia Mountain to the north and Norumbega Mountain on the other side of the sound to the northeast.

The trail descends steeply toward Valley Cove and turns left (northwest) along the shore. At about 0.7 mile, after crossing a creek that leads to the sound, you will pass a junction with the gravel Valley Cove Road. Continuing along the cove's rocky shore, the Flying Mountain Trail crosses huge boulders and rock faces. Pink granite steps bring you over some of the biggest slabs. At one spot, particularly treacherous when wet, you need to carefully make your way over a rock face to the top of a series of stone steps. The steps are held against the side of a cliff only with iron rods.

Beyond Valley Cove, one more series of stone steps brings you up and over rocky cliffs. The trail then gets relatively flat. A long series of log bridges takes you across a boggy area. You will soon cross a cool creek meandering into Somes Sound and climb a rocky ledge that offers views of St. Sauveur Mountain and a last glimpse of the sound.

At 1.6 miles, you will reach a major intersection where trails diverge to Acadia Mountain, Valley Peak, St. Sauveur Mountain, and Man O' War Truck Road.

The Flying Mountain Trail officially ends here. Return the way you came for a 3.2-mile round trip.

Options: For a 1.5-mile loop that skips the rocky shore of Valley Cove, turn left (southeast) at 0.7 mile, at the junction with the gravel Valley Cove Road. Follow the road back 0.8 mile to the parking area.

For an ambitious 4.7-mile loop that circles back on the St. Sauveur Trail over St. Sauveur Mountain, turn left (northwest) at 1.7 miles, onto the gravel Man O' War Truck Road. In another 0.8 mile, turn left (southwest) at the junction with the Acadia Mountain Trail. Stay straight as the trail joins the St. Sauveur Trail, leading over St. Sauveur Mountain and onto Valley Peak in another 1.6 miles. Bear right (south) at Valley Peak, on to the Valley Peak Trail, and descend 0.4 mile southwest to the gravel Valley Cove Road. Turn right (south) on the gravel road, returning to the parking area in another 0.2 mile.

17
BEECH CLIFF TRAIL

Highlights: Enjoy cliff-top views of Echo Lake and beyond. This trail may be closed from spring to late summer during peregrine falcon breeding season.
Type of hike: Loop.
Total distance: 0.8 mile.
Map: USGS Acadia National Park and Vicinity.
Parking and trailhead facilities: There are no facilities at the Beech Mountain parking lot.

Finding the trailhead: Head south from Somesville on Maine 102, and turn right (west) at the flashing yellow light toward Pretty Marsh. Take the second left on to Beech Hill Road, at a sign pointing to Beech Mountain and Beech Cliff. Follow Beech Hill Road south for 3.2 miles to the parking lot at its end. The trailhead leaves from across the parking lot, on the left (east) side of the road.

Key points:
0.0 Beech Cliff Trailhead.
0.2 At the junction with Canada Cliffs Trail, bear left (northeast) to Beech Cliff loop.
0.3 Reach Beech Cliff.
0.6 To close the loop, bear right (southwest) back to the parking area.

Beech Cliff Trail
Beech Mountain Trail

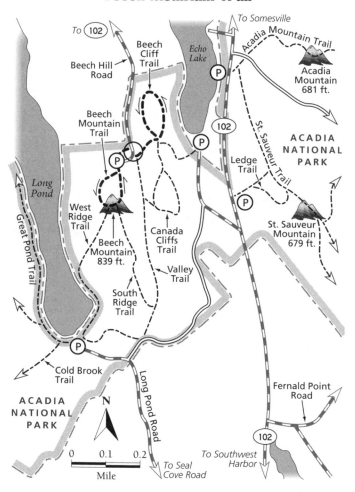

The hike: This is the easier of two ways to access Beech Cliff and its views, because the trailhead is basically at the same elevation as the cliff.

From the parking area, the trail rises gradually through the woods to a junction with the Canada Cliffs Trail at 0.2 mile. Bear left (northeast) to the Beech Cliff loop, where you have a choice of taking the inland or the cliff side of the loop. Either way is relatively flat, with some granite steps to make the footing easier. To get the views first, bear right on the cliff-side half of the loop, reaching Beech Cliff at 0.3 mile. From here, you can look down on Echo Lake Beach and the Appalachian Mountain Club (AMC) Camp—but do not get too close to the edge. Acadia and St. Sauveur Mountains are farther east. To the south are Somes Sound, the Gulf of Maine, and the Cranberry Isles. And to the southwest is Beech Mountain, with its fire tower. You may also hear the traffic on ME 102, across the lake.

The trail continues along the cliff, then circles inland, closing the loop at 0.6 mile. Bear right (southwest) to return to the parking area at 0.8 mile.

Option: After closing the Beech Cliff loop, turn left (south) on the Canada Cliffs Trail to add a 1-mile loop. You will come to two trail junctions on the Canada Cliffs ridge. The first one leads left (east) down to Echo Lake; stay straight on the ridge. The second leads right (southwest) off the ridge; bear left (southeast). The trail finally circles west and down off the ridge. Continue straight (northwest) at the next junction, and then go right (north) at the final junction to return to the Beech Mountain parking area.

18
BEECH MOUNTAIN TRAIL

see map page 70

Highlights: This trail offers views of Long Pond, Somes Sound, and the surrounding scenery from 839-foot Beech Mountain, which is topped by a fire tower.

Type of hike: Loop.

Total distance: 1.1 mile.

Map: USGS Acadia National Park and Vicinity.

Parking and trailhead facilities: The Beech Mountain parking lot has no facilities.

Finding the trailhead: Head south from Somesville on Maine 102, and turn right (west) at the flashing yellow light toward Pretty Marsh. Take the second left onto Beech Hill Road, at a sign pointing to Beech Mountain and Beech Cliff. Follow Beech Hill Road south for 3.2 miles to the parking lot at its end. The trailhead is at the northwest end of the parking lot.

Key points:

0.0 Beech Mountain Trailhead.

0.1 Bear right (southwest) at the fork, going around the loop counterclockwise.

0.6 At the junction with the Beech Mountain West Ridge Trail, bear left (east).

0.7 Reach the Beech Mountain summit. At the Beech Mountain South Ridge Trail junction, bear left (north).

The hike: Beech Mountain rises from a thin peninsula-like ridge of land sandwiched between Long Pond and Echo Lake, providing views all around. The 839-foot peak is also distinctive for its fire tower—the only mountain in Acadia to have one—and is a good place from which to watch the migration of hawks. In fact, we saw four kestrels dive and soar above us when we hiked on the mountain one fall.

At 0.1 mile, where the Beech Mountain Trail forks, bear right (southwest) to head the easier way (counterclockwise) around the loop up to the summit. You will soon get spectacular views of Long Pond to the right (west) of the wide-open trail. At 0.6 mile, reach the junction with the Beech Mountain West Ridge Trail. Bear left (east). A series of log stairs leads to the summit.

At 0.7 mile, reach the steel fire tower atop Beech Mountain, and the junction with the Beech Mountain South Ridge Trail. Access to the deck of the U.S. government-owned fire tower is blocked, but you can climb to the first platform and enjoy its almost 360-degree views of the ocean and surrounding mountains. Echo Lake, Acadia Mountain, and St. Sauveur Mountain are to the east, while Southwest Harbor, Northeast Harbor, and the Cranberry Isles are to the southeast, and Long Pond is to the west.

The loop trail heads down quickly to the left (northeast) along the rough mountain face. Descend along switchbacks, open cliff face, and through boulder fields. Pass what must be an erratic—an out-of-place boulder deposited by retreating glaciers. Go down a series of stone steps, then log steps. Bear right (north) at the fork, and return to the parking area at 1.1 miles.

Great Pond Trail

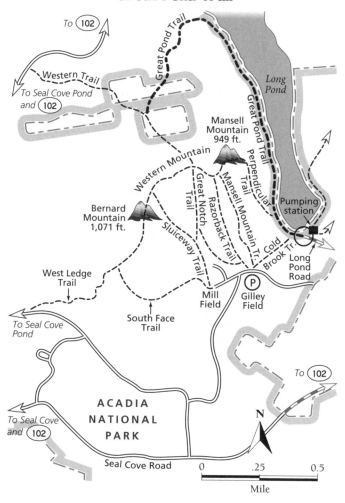

To (102)

Great Pond Trail

Western Trail

To Seal Cove Pond
and (102)

Long Pond

Great Pond Trail

Mansell
Mountain
949 ft.

Western Mountain

Perpendicular Trail

Great Notch Trail

Mansell Mountain Tr.

Razorback Trail

Bernard
Mountain
1,071 ft.

Pumping
station

Sluiceway Trail

Cold Brook Tr.

Long Pond Road

West Ledge
Trail

Mill
Field

P
Gilley Field

To Seal Cove
Pond

South Face
Trail

To Seal Cove
and (102)

To (102)

ACADIA
NATIONAL
PARK

N

Seal Cove Road

0   .25   0.5

Mile

19
GREAT POND TRAIL

Highlights: This is a mostly flat walk along the southwest shore of Long (Great) Pond, the largest body of fresh water on Mount Desert Island.

Type of hike: Out-and-back, or part of a loop up Western Mountain.

Total distance: 5.8 miles, or 4.7-mile loop.

Map: USGS Acadia National Park and Vicinity.

Parking and trailhead facilities: Park at the Long Pond pumping station. There are no facilities.

Finding the trailhead: From Southwest Harbor, head north about 0.5 mile on Maine 102. Turn left (west) at Seal Cove Road, and travel for about 0.5 mile. Head right (north) on Long Pond Road to its end at a pumping station on the shore of the pond. The trailhead is to the left (west) of the pumping station.

Key points:

0.0 Begin at the Great Pond Trailhead, and the junction with Cold Brook Trail.

0.2 Pass the junction with the Perpendicular Trail.

2.9 Reach the junction with the Western Trail.

5.8 Return to the trailhead.

The hike: The Great Pond Trail is a pleasant walk that offers the possibility of sunning on big, flat rocks, or seeing dozens of herring gulls soar on the wind above what is known as Long or Great Pond. The trail can also serve as a jumping off point for some of the challenging hikes up Western Mountain.

The trail heads left (west) from the pumping station. Cold Brook Trail goes inland, while the Great Pond Trail stays along the shore. At 0.2 mile, the Perpendicular Trail heads steeply up toward the twin wooded summits—Mansell and Bernard—that make up Western Mountain. Continue straight (north) on the Great Pond Trail.

Farther along the shore, there are large, flat rocks suitable for sunning. We saw a huge flock of herring gulls soar on the wind here.

While the beginning of the trail is well graded, roots and rocks make the footing a bit more difficult farther in. Most people don't venture this far. As the trail hits its northernmost point, it heads inland and up the northern shoulder of Western Mountain. At one point, the trail crosses a creek on a long log bridge.

At 2.9 miles, the trail ends at the junction with the Western Trail. Return the way you came.

Options: To do a 4.7-mile loop back via 949-foot Mansell Mountain, go 0.4 mile southeast on the Western Mountain Trail from its junction with the Great Pond Trail, heading farther up the northern shoulder of Western Mountain to the Great Notch. Turn left (east) for 0.3 mile over the wooded summit of Mansell Mountain, and then down the 0.9-mile Perpendicular Trail. Turn right (south) at the shore of the pond and go 0.2 mile to return to the pumping station parking area.

Wonderland Trail
Ship Harbor Nature Trail

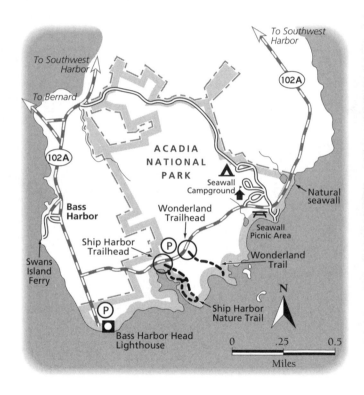

To Southwest Harbor

To Southwest Harbor

102A

To Bernard

102A

Bass Harbor

ACADIA NATIONAL PARK

Seawall Campground

Natural seawall

Wonderland Trailhead

Seawall Picnic Area

Ship Harbor Trailhead

P

Wonderland Trail

Swans Island Ferry

P

Bass Harbor Head Lighthouse

Ship Harbor Nature Trail

N

0   .25   0.5

Miles

BASS HARBOR AREA

20
WONDERLAND TRAIL

Highlights: You can explore pink granite outcrops along the shore, and tide pools at low tide.
Type of hike: Out-and-back.
Total distance: 1.4 miles.
Map: USGS Acadia National Park and Vicinity.
Parking and trailhead facilities: Trailhead parking lot on the left, or south side of Maine 102A.

Finding the trailhead: From Southwest Harbor, head south about 1 mile on Maine 102. Bear left (southeast) on Maine 102A, passing the town of Manset in about 1 mile, Seawall Campground and picnic area in about 3 miles, and reaching the Wonderland Trailhead in about 4 miles. The trailhead is on the left (southeast) side of the road.

Key points:
0.0 Wonderland Trailhead.
0.1 The trail heads slightly uphill.

0.7 Reach the rocky shoreline.
1.4 Return to the trailhead.

The hike: Once you see the smooth pink granite along the shore, smell the salty sea, and explore the tide pools, you will know why they call this the Wonderland Trail.

The easy trail along an old gravel road starts by winding through dark woods, but a huge smooth pink granite rock on the left soon hints at the picture show to come.

At about 0.1 mile, go up a slight hill and make your way carefully among some roots and rocks. This is the toughest part of an otherwise very easy, well-graded trail. Skunk cabbage is found along this section of the trail, with its distinctive purplish-red leaves and yellow flower in early spring, and huge green foliage in summer.

Through the trees, you begin to see the ocean on the right (southeast). At 0.7 mile, the trail brings you to the shore, where the pink granite dramatically meets the sea.

You can spend hours exploring here, especially when low tide exposes tide pools and their diverse marine life, from rockweed to barnacles to green crabs. Be careful of wet rocks, slick seaweed, and sudden waves.

Return the way you came.

21
SHIP HARBOR
NATURE TRAIL

see map page 78

Highlights: This trail features pink granite cliffs along shoreline.

Type of hike: Loop.

Total distance: 1.3 miles.

Map: USGS Acadia National Park and Vicinity.

Parking and trailhead facilities: The trailhead parking lot is on the left (south) side of Maine 102A. There is a chemical toilet at the trailhead.

Finding the trailhead: From Southwest Harbor, head south about 1 mile on Maine 102. Bear left (southeast) on Maine 102A, passing the town of Manset in about 1 mile, Seawall Campground and picnic area in about 3 miles, and the Wonderland Trail parking area in about 4 miles. Ship Harbor Trailhead is about 0.2 mile beyond the Wonderland Trailhead.

Key points:

0.0 Ship Harbor Nature Trailhead.

0.1 Bear left (southeast) at the first fork.

0.3 At the three-way intersection, bear left (southeast) up the hill.

0.6 The trail meets the shoreline; bear right (north) along the Ship Harbor channel.

1.0 At the three-way intersection, bear left (northwest) along Ship Harbor.
1.2 Bear left (northwest) at the fork.
1.3 Complete the loop.

The hike: The drama of the sea crashing against the pink granite cliffs of Acadia is the greatest reward of this easy trail. But there are also other, smaller pleasures, like seeing ocean ducks known as common eiders floating at the mouth of Ship Harbor, or watching a red squirrel gnaw on a nut, as we did one day.

This interpretive nature trail—the descriptive brochure is available at the park visitor center for 50 cents—brings visitors to 14 different signposts, which provide lessons on the glacial action that carved out Mount Desert Island; spruce and tamarack trees; the pink granite cliffs; and the local legend that explains the name Ship Harbor. Although the loop trail is easy, footing is rough, with roots and rocks in places, and hills in others. Wear appropriate footwear.

The trail, built in 1957, begins with a view of the harbor in the distance, and a sign marking the apple trees of a farm that once stood here.

At the first fork, at 0.1 mile, bear left (southeast) to follow the numbered signposts through the woods. Soon after signpost 4, at 0.3 mile, you will come to a three-way intersection. Bear left (southeast) up the hill to follow the signposts in order. (If the uphill presents too much of an obstacle, you can take the middle path southwest to the shoreline instead, and backtrack on the return to avoid the hill altogether.)

Whether you climb the hill or take the easier middle path, you will come to dramatic pink cliffs at about 0.6 mile. You can spend hours exploring the shoreline, especially at low tide, when barnacles, rockweed, snails, and other sea life are exposed by the receding waters.

Loop back (north) along the channel leading into Ship Harbor, until you return to the three-way intersection again, at about 1 mile. Follow the arrow on the signpost to the left (northwest) to get to the final leg of the loop trail, which brings you along Ship Harbor. Legend says that during the Revolutionary War, an American ship escaping a British gunboat got stuck in the mud here—hence the name Ship Harbor.

After the last signpost, 14, at 1.2 miles, you will come to another fork in the trail. Bear left (northwest) and you will be back at the parking lot.

About the Authors

Dolores Kong and Dan Ring have backpacked all 270 miles of the Appalachian Trail in Maine, and have been hiking and backpacking together for years in New England and elsewhere. Dolores is a reporter at the *Boston Globe,* and Dan is Statehouse Bureau Chief in Boston for the *Union-News* of Springfield, Mass. They are married and live outside Boston.